MW00465829

Freedom to Love

After the Hurt

By

Michelle A. Smullen

Copyright © 2020 Michelle Smullen. *Freedom to Love After the Hurt*.

All rights reserved. No part of this publication may be reproduced, distributed, or transmitted in any form or by any means, including photocopying, recording, or other electronic or mechanical methods, without the prior written permission of the publisher, except in the case of brief quotations embodied in critical reviews and certain other noncommercial uses permitted by copyright law. For permission requests, write to the publisher, addressed "Attention: Permissions Coordinator," at the address below.

Contribution by Kiyanni Bryan, Write It Out Publishing LLC in the United States of America.

Illustrator: Ronda Flynn WOW, Inc.

Editor: Katherine A. Young

ISBN: 978-1- 7356619-0-2 (Paperback)

First Printing, 2020.

Michelle Andrews Smullen

Virginia Beach, VA 23464

Email: iam@michelleasmullen.com

www.michelleasmullen.com

Dedication

Dear Ma and Da

Thank you for training me up in the way that I should go and never giving up on me when I made mistakes along the way. Introducing me to God and having a life with Jesus Christ, is the best gift ever! I know the Lord's face shines on me from heaven even brighter because you are there. I will love you forever.

With All My Heart,

Michelle, your favorite knee-baby.

FOREWORD

Love is: patient, and kind, and it's not envious, it doesn't boast, its not proud, it does not dishonor others, it's not self-seeking, it's not easily angered, it does not keep records of wrongs, it is happy about the truth, it always protects, always trusts, always hopes, always preservers because love never fails.

Hmmmp...but what if love does fail? Like, what if love isn't so patient and kind, and jealousy creeps in, or it does get mad, and dishonors someone, or disregards someone, and score cards are kept, and it's wrapped in lies and deceit, and it doesn't protect, and trust is broken, and you have no hope to preserve? What if all the love that two people shared did fail...then what?

Sometimes life comes at us fast, real fast. When we are faced with difficult situations and circumstances, especially as it relates to matters of the heart, oftentimes we find ourselves fumbling around in a foggy valley. In that valley, it's hard as hell to see, you aren't sure which way to go because this place is not familiar, you don't feel safe, you don't feel protected. But for me, one of the worst things about being in that valley is not being able to catch my breath - whew chile the air is dark and thick. I seem to choke on the difficult situations and circumstances that life has now presented me with. So I stand there in that dark, foggy valley struggling to see, struggling to breathe - trying so very hard to just catch my breath. Now I know I'm not the only one who has experienced some valley moments in life; stuck, begging God to take all the pain away, and thinking why would God bring me to this place that I absolutely hate - WHY?

But just like the good father that he is, after a while of allowing me to try to figure out which way to go on my own, He gives me a "nudge": turn this way, stop, take a deep breath, look over there there's some fresh water. Those "nudges" remind me that God is right there with me in that valley, He's actually been with me the entire time. Those nudges also remind me that if I just invite Him into those difficult situations and circumstances, He will take care of me and all the hard life stuff. So I make a step towards surrender to what God's plan is for those valley moments...those moments when love does fail. Though we do not understand why and how and what to do, one thing we can be forever sure of is:

The Lord is my shepherd, I lack nothing,

He gives me rest in green pastures,

He leads me beside quiet waters, and He restores my whole soul,

He guides me along the right paths because He is a good, good father

And when I find myself in those dark valley moments, I don't have to fear because He's right there with me protecting and comforting me

Those who meant me evil, God will turn it around for my good and they will have a front row seat to watch

He anoints my head with oil, and my cup overflows

He assures me that goodness and love will follow me for the rest of my life

And that I will dwell in His house forever

Now to answer the question, what do you do if love fails? I simply hear God saying TRUST ME.

So when Michelle shared her story and her heart in Freedom to Love After the Hurt, I found encouragement, healing, and a tremendous amount of hope in her testimony of overcoming. If you are currently walking through a valley moment in your life, I pray this testimony provides a glimmer of hope for you in whatever circumstances you may be facing. But I am certain this heartfelt book will show you that absolutely nothing is too hard for God, if we simply TRUST HIM.

Ronda Flynn

Preface

It was September 2006 when the spirit of infidelity had been unveiled. My marriage as I knew it had come to a place that I could have never prepared myself for and our relationship had forever been changed. It literally took my breath away to know that my husband, my high school sweetheart, and my best friend had indeed been unfaithful to me. The sickening feeling in the pit of my stomach was now a reality for me; for us.

Undoubtedly, his infidelity went against everything God ordained in marriage, but I will never forget the day God whispered to me "if you just hold on, I will make it alright". It was a gentle desperation in those words that I knew God was fighting for us. That whisper felt safe and while I believed with everything within me that God was able to heal our brokenness and restore our marriage, I just couldn't grasp "the how"...How could I ever overcome the fear to love my husband freely without looking over my shoulder every day and just going through the motions; portraying an image of what trust and forgiveness is supposed to look like?

There I was wrestling with God because I was just too hurt to allow myself to even see the possibility of how to overcome the heart wrenching fear I was facing. For as much as I wanted it all to be undone, it was in this season of my life that I discovered that God's grace is sufficient, and His power is made perfect in my weakness. All I needed to do was hold on.

Table of Contents

I. Introduction   1

II. Overcoming Hurt Through Prayer and God's Word   3

   A. Forgiveness   3

   B. Truth   8

   C. Betrayal   11

   D. Healing   16

III. Fighting for Your Marriage   27

   A. Reasons to Fight   27

   B. Reasons Not to Fight   30

IV. Is Divorce an Option?   37

   A. Biblical Grounds for Divorce   37

   B. How Divorce Affects the Children   39

   C. Hope in Separation   42

   D. Renewed Commitment   48

V. Sexual Transparency   53

   A. Choices   53

   B. Effective Communication   56

VI. Statistics   61

   A. Divorce and Adultery   61

   B. Religion and Infidelity   63

VII. Interviews & Testimonies   65

   A. Do You Think You Could Love Freely in Your Marriage After Being Hurt by Infidelity?   65

B. How Has Infidelity Impacted Your Life Now?   66

VIII. Setting Boundaries   71

    A. Should You Set Boundaries with Your Spouse?   71

    B. Addressing the Fear   72

    C. Expectancy   74

IX. Conclusion   81

    A New Beginnings   81

Bibliography   87

I. Introduction

Can you overcome the fear to love freely in your marriage after the hurt infidelity has caused? Through the Word of God, personal experience, and cited resources, I will present a pathway to overcoming the fear to love freely after the hurt. *"For God hath not given us the spirit of fear; but of power and of love, and of a sound mind" (2 Timothy 1:17 KJV)*. When two people are joined together in marriage, it is never with the intention of being separated or divorced, not to mention because of infidelity. According to Webster's dictionary, infidelity in this instance is described as: "unfaithfulness to a moral obligation; disloyalty; the act or fact of having a romantic or sexual relationship with someone other than one's husband, wife, or partner."

These attributes of infidelity can leave a person feeling hopeless. The hurt feels unbearable and you have every reason to let go, but you can't. *Will I ever get past the hurt?* On this journey to freedom, one must pray and meditate on the word of God daily, discuss the reasons to fight for your marriage versus the reasons not to fight, weigh the options of divorce, have sexual transparency, and set boundaries. Being in bondage is never God's will for our life. We are more than conquerors! *"The Lord shall fight for you, and ye shall hold your peace" (Exodus 14:14, KJV).*

II. Overcoming Hurt Through Prayer and God's Word

A. Forgiveness

The most important step in the journey to overcome fear in order to love freely is forgiveness. *"Be kind and compassionate to one another, forgiving each other, just as in Christ God forgave you"* *Ephesians 4:32 (NIV)*. Healing, restoration, renewing, or overcoming cannot take place without genuine forgiveness. Those who are children of God understand that it is necessary to forgive when we have been hurt because if we don't, our Father will not forgive us. However, many people don't understand the importance of forgiveness because they have not been taught what the Word of God says about it. The assumption is to forgive if you choose to and you don't if you choose not to. This brings another element to forgiveness on the journey to overcome because not everyone who is married are believers, let alone have given their lives to Christ. Therefore, it is very important to understand that marriage is a covenant ordained by God and because of this alone, it will only endure on the foundation in which He has made. His principles must be applied to a union He instituted.

> *"And the rib, which the Lord God had taken from man, made him a woman, and brought her unto the man. And Adam said, 'This is now bone of my bones, and flesh of my flesh: she shall be called Woman, because she was taken out of Man.' Therefore, shall a man leave his father and his mother, and shall cleave unto his wife: and they shall be one flesh" Genesis 2:22-24 (KJV).*

Biblically, forgiveness seems easier to fathom as it relates to our obedience to God; regrettably, it can be the most difficult to achieve. In our flesh, we feel justified in being angry, bitter, confused, and simply hurt. It seems unfair to expect any kindness or compassion towards someone who has been unfaithful when they vowed that they would be. We want to apply our own feelings about the situation, and still have our sins excused; unfortunately, we must apply the entire Word of God and look to Him as our example.

God did not wait on us to apologize for our sins; instead, He introduced forgiveness to us. Our debt has been canceled and we are free. True forgiveness occurs when we decide to cancel the debt of our spouse's infidelity, irrespective of whether they confess their actions were wrong. There are many instances where an apology is never said; rather, it is implied. This can be very difficult for the hurting spouse to accept because it seems like the "least they could do was apologize." Moreover, true forgiveness comes unattached to anything and is completely unconfined to anything we think is owed to us or [1]deserve as "punishment". Forgiveness is not for the person who caused the offense, but truly for the person who has been hurt.

"How is forgiveness even possible with all the hurt I feel?" This is a very real emotion and a very common question you may ask yourself on the journey to overcome the fear to love freely. The infidelity cannot be erased. The pain of it all cannot be erased. You can't act as if it did not happen or that the

---

[1] Farley and Millard. (2013) The Hurt and the Healer.

hurt is not real. Evaluating the emotional hurt is imperative as emotions themselves are not sin. *"In your anger do not sin: Do not let the sun go down while you are still angry," (Ephesians 4:26 NIV).* This evaluation requires the spouse who has been hurt to be honest with their feelings and not suppress them.

At all costs, true forgiveness cannot be manipulated and is not conditional. Specifically, it cannot come with the expectation that your spouse will be forthcoming with the details of the adulterous relationship once you have "forgiven" them. This expectation could lead to a backwards step if your spouse chooses not to share in the way you were seeking. An emotional rollercoaster is not God's intention; therefore, you cannot create your own terms and pray for God's help to forgive. His will is genuine forgiveness. Our prayers matter to God and He wants us to be free to make the choice to forgive on this journey of overcoming.

We must seek the willingness to forgive and the courage to release the debt you feel your spouse owes you. We must pray for understanding of the Word of God and acceptance of what it says. Ask God to give you a heart of genuine forgiveness; it can begin the healing process for the unfaithful spouse who may also be hurting. The power of forgiveness is amazing!

B. Truth

Does the truth matter when you realize and have accepted that it was never God's plan for your marriage to end? Realistically, you may never know all the details of your spouse's infidelity to decipher what is true (fact or reality) and what isn't true. Continuing to search for the truth in the details of the adulterous relationship robs you of your peace and strength because it keeps you confused, angry, bitter, resentful, in fear of being alone, continually blaming yourself, and remaining in a state of shock over and over again. *"But when he, the Spirit of truth, comes, he will guide you into all the truth. He will not speak on his own; he will speak only what he hears, and he will tell you what is yet to come"* (John 16:13 NIV). Overcoming will not be achieved by searching for the truth in the details of the adulterous relationship. It will only be achieved in seeking after God through prayer for peace whether you know the truth or not and for strength to accept the truth He reveals. *Isaiah 26:3* encourages us that those whose minds stay on the

LORD will be kept in perfect peace because we trust in Him.

In exploring the concept of truth, it is necessary to understand that truth originated from the character, the mind, the will, the glory, and existence of God. Truth may be characterized as the [2] "self-expression of God" and because the truth is derived from God, it is theological. *"He is the Rock, his work is perfect: for all his ways are judgment: a God of truth and without iniquity, just and right is he"* *(Deuteronomy 32:4 KJV).* While it is important to expect the truth, it is more important to know that the nature of God will never lead you into what is not true. Overcoming is not contingent on whether your

---

[2] What is Truth? www.gty.org.

spouse has been completely truthful about their infidelity if your trust is in God, who is truth.

The word of God assures us in *Numbers 23:19* that He is not a man that He should lie or like a human that he will change his mind. He fulfills every promise! It is not possible for God to lie. Therefore, in order to overcome the fear to love freely, you must remain prayerful and meditate on the word of God daily. Your mind must stay on God alone with intentions of allowing the Holy Spirit to guide you through the desire to decipher the truth from a situation created by human decisions.

C. Betrayal

The word *Betrayal* has always had a "haunting" connotation to me. It is as if someone was lurking around waiting for the opportunity to inflict pain. While causing pain may not have been the intent, it occurs inevitably when there is infidelity. Betrayal is more than just lying. This breach of trust makes overcoming seem as though it is too impossible to achieve. Often the haunting thought of the betrayal is what causes thoughts of revenge. You want your spouse to hurt just as much as you hurt. You want them to feel what disloyalty feels like. You may have thoughts of causing physical harm or thoughts of being unfaithful yourself. In times of desperation to overcome the hurt, spouses will even use their children as manipulation because they know this will cause pain for sure. As much as you may think it will free you from the hurt, it only adds links to the chain.

Agreeably, the feeling of betrayal is heart-wrenching, and a feeling of emptiness; however, we must recognize that betrayal is derived from evil. [3]Satan deceived Eve and he was able to convince her to question the instruction [4]God told Adam not to eat from the tree of knowledge of good and evil or he would surely die. I used to think Satan was the betrayer because of his deception, but he had no loyalty to Adam and Eve. His intent was of evil to cause them to fall. In reality, they unintentionally allowed this act of evil to cause them to betray God as their loyalty was to Him.

The Apostle Paul urges to remind us in *Ephesians 6*, that "*we do not wrestle against flesh and blood. Instead, against the principalities, against powers, against rulers of darkness of this world, against spiritual wickedness in high places.*" This

---

[3] Genesis 3:4-5
[4] Genesis 2:16-17

concept is difficult to apply to our life when flesh and blood is the actual cause of the betrayal. This passage of scripture also instructs us to put on the full armor of God so that we are able to stand against the evil schemes of the devil. Simply stated, our struggle is not with our unfaithful spouse. Our struggle is with the spirit of betrayal. The hurt and the sting of devastation caused by betrayal cannot be overcome with fleshly weapons, but mighty through God for the bringing down of strongholds (refer to *2 Corinthians 10:4).*

The Word of God is our guide and prayer is our greatest weapon of warfare. We must be intentional about believing what it says and strategic in our prayers against the enemy. Our flesh simply cannot withstand evil. We are spiritual beings and must learn what it takes to remain victorious over the feeling betrayal brings. We must pray that our heart will not hold on to vengeance because it belongs to the Lord. We must pray against the schemes of the devil. We must pray against the wickedness lurking to destroy our marriages and cause division in our families. Overcoming the betrayal might seem impossible, but with God all things are possible.

D. Healing

Working in the medical field, I have learned many different aspects of healing. No one person is the same and requires different solutions to their healing. Of all that I have learned about healing, one aspect that has remained the same is that healing comes from the inside out. A cast may be used to hold a broken bone in place, but the cast does not promote the healing process that takes place in the body. Recently, a young lady had surgery on her foot. At her follow-up appointment, one of the areas around one of the screws placed in her foot was infected. She had been given antibiotics to take after the surgery as a precaution; therefore, they were watching this infected area very closely. She shared with me she had not been eating very much because she did not have an appetite. My response to her was "How do you expect to heal properly if you don't eat?"

Healing from infidelity can feel like a tug of war. It is a struggle to find healing. It takes so much strength to pull the rope from the side of hurt. Some days, it's a fight just to think clearly, but you build up enough strength and the hurt is almost over the line to healing... then BAM! Hurt takes a big yank and you almost fall over the line, but somehow you manage not to go over it. You think *Do I have any tears left to cry?* but they continue to fall. The thought of it all keeps replaying in your mind, but your heart really does want to be free; you want the cast to come off once and for all! You have come to a place where you are tired of feeling like you are not in control. You are beginning to desire the feeling of normalcy again. You are willing to take the steps toward restoring your marriage. But you can't seem to conquer the thoughts and you're back to wondering why it had to happen. You have considered letting your spouse in a little more than you did a few days ago, but the thoughts will not let you. The truth is, this tug-of-war going on is not of God and the power is within us to conquer these thoughts and make them obey God. The word of God says:

> We demolish arguments and every pretension that sets itself up against the knowledge of God, and we take captive every thought to make it obedient to Christ" (2 Corinthians 10:5 NIV).

"People are disturbed not by things, but by the views they take of them." -Epictetus (Subotnik, 2005). As much as we "just want to be better," the reality is that it takes time to heal. While on the journey to overcome the fear to love freely, it is important to realize that a loss or lack of some sort has occurred in your marriage. In the book, *Surviving Infidelity: Making Decisions, Recovering from the Pain,* the five stages of grief and loss were discussed as part of the strategy to help married couples cope with the pain thus heal from infidelity. These stages may not all occur in this order.

Stage 1: Denial

It doesn't seem real and you can't believe it is happening to you. You keep thinking when you wake up, it will all have been a dream. You are in a state of disbelief and your body tries to find a way to protect itself and denial is the answer.

Stage 2: Anger

It is in this stage that you go beyond being angry to being in rage. Episodes of screaming and crying may occur just at the thought of your unfaithful spouse. This is the stage where thoughts of revenge may take place and are often carried out. You are moving through the process when you can recognize your anger and convey it in a safe manner.

Stage 3: Bargaining

After the anger dissolves, you may begin to bargain as you face the reality that the infidelity is real, and your marriage needs help. You may find yourself going above and beyond to please your spouse in areas you have been lacking in. Your focus may be to do all that you can to make them happy. It is very important not to be fooled into thinking you must condone their behavior if you know the affair has not ended.

Stage 4: Depression

In this stage, the infidelity may take a toll on you physically, mentally, and psychologically. You may cry a lot and your appetite may increase or decrease. You may experience insomnia and lack of energy to do anything. You work because the bills still need to be paid. You are caring for the children because they can't take care of themselves. Outside of these things, nothing else really seems to matter. Contemplating suicide may occur in this stage.

Stage 5: Acceptance

Healing cannot be achieved without acceptance. Comprehending what has happened is intellectual acceptance. Verbalizing what has happened without the penetrating response is emotional acceptance, which occurs later in the process. This stage may seem very unattainable because many people feel and verbalize, they will never accept what has taken place in their life. However, acceptance is not giving permission for infidelity, rather, it is acknowledging the infidelity has taken place. The result of not accepting is resentment and failure to trust again. Acceptance is not optional if you want to overcome the fear to love freely in your marriage.

Date_____

Dear God,

   "Because of the LORD's great love, we are not
consumed, for his compassions never fail. They are
new every morning; great is your faithfulness"
(Lamentations 3:22-23 NIV).

_____

_____

_____

_____

_____

_____

_____

_____

_____

_____

_____

_____

_____

_____

_____

_____

_____

I smile today because...

III. Fighting for Your Marriage

A. Reasons to Fight

"Something inside of me was against all that I was experiencing; for as much as I was going through, it just didn't feel right not to fight." In my fight for my marriage, there was never a time I wanted to let go. I thought that letting go was what I was going to have to do, but I never wanted to. It just didn't feel right. I knew in my heart what God had promised me, had promised us. I came to the realization that after we were married, I didn't understand that there was an "essence" to be married. It wasn't just two people who loved each other decided to make it official because they had a child and it was the right thing to do. There is a way in which God intended marriage to be. Apostle Paul puts it this way:

"Therefore, I do not run like someone running aimlessly; I do not fight like a boxer beating the air. No, I strike a blow to my body and make it my slave so that after I have preached to others, I myself will not be disqualified for the prize" (1 Corinthians 9:26-27 NIV).

I wanted the prize at the end and I realized that the only way I was going to get the prize was to stay in the fight. But what were my reasons?

I always encourage my children, especially my 19-year-old daughter, to evaluate the reasons why they are making the decisions they are making. Is it just because everyone else is doing it? Does it just seem like the right thing to do for the time being? Are you making that decision because you are tired of waiting for your expected result? Perhaps some of the decisions may seem right until you begin evaluating the reasons you are making them. As we may expect honesty (speaking without intent to deceive) from our spouse, it is much more important to be honest (and not deceive) ourselves. Knowing the reasons why we are choosing to fight for our marriage is a crucial part of overcoming the fear to love freely.

- It is in the will of God that our marriage survives.
- My children are a reason to fight for my marriage.
- I still love my husband is my reason to fight for my marriage.
- I still love my wife is my reason to fight for my marriage.
- I know they still love me is a reason to fight for my marriage.

- I have forgiven.

- I feel they are genuinely sorry for the hurt they have caused.

- I do not want to be alone is a reason to fight for my marriage.

- I did not get married to get divorced.

- My husband/wife asked me not to give up on them.

- Believing God can restore our marriage is a reason to fight for my marriage.

- A child born because of the adulterous relationship may be a reason to fight.

B. Reasons Not to Fight

"Are you still in love with me?" This was the question I asked my husband one day while talking on the phone. This was before I officially found out he had been unfaithful. Although I knew something had changed, I was not prepared for the answer. "I don't know," were his words. They cut so deep and rocked my entire soul. If I didn't know anything else, I knew he loved me. But when that became questionable, it seemed to have changed the entire dynamic of my thought process. It was almost as if I had been naïve or just didn't want to believe what I was feeling. Not that it wasn't impossible for him to be unfaithful; just the same, it was possible for me to be unfaithful also if that was my choice. The actual words were unsure, but there was something about the sound of his voice that was sure; well, at least that is what the enemy wanted me to believe.

Evaluating the reasons not to fight for your marriage or keep you from fighting is just as crucial as evaluating the reasons to fight. Often when we have been hurt because of infidelity, we compare ourselves to the person our spouse has chosen to be unfaithful with. If we ponder this thought too long, we will find ourselves going around in a circle. This will be so engraved in our minds that it may become a reason not to fight; obviously, we don't "measure up" or "have what it takes" to make our spouse happy. This is a lie! This is not a contest—it's your marriage. In a 2014 CNN report funded by the National Institute of Aging, researchers discovered that " [5]a bad marriage causes more harm to the heart than a good marriage offers positive benefits to cardiovascular health."

- An abusive spouse is a reason not to fight (emotional and physical).
- Repeated infidelity is a reason not to fight.

---

[5] www.verywellmind.com

- Not being able to get past the fear of not knowing the future with your spouse is a reason not to fight.

- A peaceful agreement that it's best to end the marriage is a reason not to fight.

- Blatant disrespect has taken place (the adulterous relationship has taken place in your home and/or around your children keep you from fighting from your marriage).

- Your spouse refuses to change is a reason not to fight for your marriage.

- A child is born because of the adulterous relationship.

- Family involvement is a reason not to fight for your marriage.

- No willingness to try to salvage the marriage is a reason not to fight for your marriage.

- Lack of remorse about the infidelity is a reason

  not to fight for your marriage.

Date_____

Dear God,

"When I tried to understand it all, I just couldn't. It

was too puzzling—too much of a riddle to me"

(Psalm 73:16 TPT).

_____

_____

_____

_____

_____

_____

_____

_____

_____

_____

_____

_____

_____

_____

_____

_____

_____

_____

I smile today because...

IV. Is Divorce an Option?

A. Biblical Grounds for Divorce

Divorce is always an option as you cannot force anyone to stay married if they choose not to. Whether it's the right option is the better question. Searching the answer to this question leads to transparency. There are many factors to consider when contemplating divorce because of infidelity. One major factor is considering what the Bible says about divorce.

> *"It has been said, 'Anyone who divorces his wife must give her a certificate of divorce.'[a] 32 But I tell you that anyone who divorces his wife, except for sexual immorality, makes her the victim of*

adultery, and anyone who marries a divorced woman commits adultery" (Matthew 5:31-32 NIV).

Divorce is division within a union God instituted; therefore, this is never a part of the plan. What God has joined together let no man put asunder. The truth is that divorce happens amongst believers as well as unbelievers, but this is not to be thought of as the "norm."

B. How Divorce Affects the Children

The following information are the results of research comparing children of divorced parents to children with married parents. *How Could Divorce Affect My Kids* by Amy Desai, J.D. research reveals:

- Children from divorced homes suffer academically. They experience high levels of behavioral problems. Their grades suffer, and they are less likely to graduate from high school.[2]

- Kids whose parents' divorce are substantially more likely to be incarcerated for committing a crime as a juvenile.[3]

- Because the custodial parent's income drops substantially after a divorce, children in divorced homes are almost five times more likely to live in poverty than are children with married parents.[4]

- Teens from divorced homes are much more likely to engage in drug and alcohol use, as well as sexual intercourse than are those from intact families.[5]

- Children from divorced homes experience illness more frequently and recover from sickness more slowly. They are also more likely to suffer child abuse.[6]

- Children of divorced parents suffer more frequently from symptoms of psychological distress. And the emotional scars of divorce last into adulthood.[7]

[6,2,3,4,5,] Desai, Amy. "How Could Divorce Affect My Kids?" Focus On the Family, 1 January 2007. https://www.focusonthefamily.com/marriage/divorce-and-infidelity/should-i-get-a-divorce/how-could-divorce-affect-my-kids.

[7]Desai, Amy. "How Could Divorce Affect My Kids?" Focus On the Family, 1 January

It amazes me (in a sense) when people divorce after 20, 30, 50 years of marriage because the kids are all grown and out of the house. They spend years and years together being unhappy—just tolerating each other because they did not want to devastate their children. But isn't there a chance the children would still be devastated? Possibly more so, but the thought is that they can probably handle it better as adults. Some people feel they don't want their children to be a statistic and put into a certain socioeconomic stereotype. The impact divorce can have on children may have life-long effects. It could trickle well into their adult lives and they may duplicate what they

2007. <https://www.focusonthefamily.com/marriage/divorce-and-infidelity/should-i-get-a-divorce/how-could-divorce-affect-my-kids.>

have seen; ultimately, they would believe that "if I get married and it doesn't work out, I can just get a divorce." This may not be true for all children as divorce affects individuals differently. Some children may choose to use their parent's divorce to strive to be the best spouse they possibly can be to avoid divorce at all costs because they know first-hand the damaging effects it may cause their children. Experience is the best teacher.

C. Hope in Separation

Separation is not always necessary and does not always occur in a marriage that has experienced infidelity where the couple has chosen to work toward a renewed commitment. However, there is hope in separation if there is willingness. Pam Moody, marriage editor for [8]*Thriving Families*, shares portions of a series inspired by Dr. Gary Chapman entitled, "Hope for the Separated." She expresses that [9]"Hope [is] essential to life. Regardless of the issue at hand or the relationship in the balance, hope is the basic ingredient that keeps us moving forward." King Solomon proclaims, *"Hope deferred maketh the heart sick: but when the desire cometh, it is a tree of life"* *(Proverbs 13:12 KJV).* Having hope makes the difference. While this is true and will lead you to being free, the reality is people don't choose to marry with a plan to divorce or separate; therefore, it is very difficult to be hopeful when the nightmare you are

---

[8] Dr. Gary Chapman. "Hope for the Separated." Thriving Families Magazine.

[9] <https://www.focusonthefamily.com/marriage/divorce-and-infidelity/hope-for-the-seperated/introduction-hope-for-the-separated.>

living was never part of the plan. So, what am I hoping for if we are separated?

Until the season of separation has come to an end, no one can ever be sure of the outcome: whether it be divorce or a renewed commitment to your marriage. Those who are faced with the question, "Do we WANT to work on our marriage?" should really be asking, "Are we WILLING to work on our marriage?" Dr. Gary Chapman, who is a family counselor, radio host, associate pastor, and author, says "A willingness to work toward reconciliation is a good place to start—regardless of where you end up." No matter the outcome, God will walk with us through the valley. Overcoming the fear to love freely requires a willingness of the heart—even if it's broken.

Most oftentimes, couples who have decided to reconcile after a period of separation, end up separated again or divorced simply because they did not effectively deal with the issues which caused the initial separation. They have chosen to reconcile primarily because they missed the physical companionship and wanted to fulfill the loneliness they were experiencing. All is well for a while, but then the thoughts of the infidelity come up and out in some way, shape, or form. If a couple has chosen to separate, it is very important to invest the time and resources (professional and/or Christian counseling, plus a positive support system) during the separation to effectively address all the issues. This is not just a time to give each other space and it is certainly not an opportunity to see if your unfaithful spouse is going to pursue you to prove how much they really want to be with you. EFFECTIVELY ADDRESS THE ISSUES!

It is vital to move toward reconciliation and a renewed commitment as this is God's desire. Unfortunately, there are times this is just not the outcome given the circumstances. Woody suggests [10]"It's important that a spouse considering separation understands that he or she has a great deal of power to change the marriage—the power of influence that needs to be exerted before giving up hope." This is a very vulnerable time and while family and friends mean well, they may drain you of the power needed to change the direction of your marriage because of their advice. In the same manner, if there are children involved, it is important to be truthful with them

---

[10] <https://www.focusonthefamily.com/marriage/divorce-and-infidelity/hope-for-the-separated/separation-as-an-act-of-love.>

about the situation at their level of understanding. Lying to them will not protect them. Both parents should tell the children together their plan to separate and the reasons why, but above all, express to them their love for them and reinforce that they are not to blame. Children should also be assured that the parents are not separating from them. This is a time for the parents to make every effort to be civil toward one another.

Be sure to seek Godly counseling, continually asking God to give you a discerning spirit. Separation may not be ideal, but it may be a necessary act of love and means of survival if the circumstances are too unbearable even after having done all you can do. If divorce is unavoidable despite giving an honest effort, you will be able to live better with the choice you have made rather than the guilt you may face with giving up too soon.

Dr. Chapman offers these suggestions to those who are separated:

- Guard your attitudes and actions; keep them positive.
- Avoid or abandon any romantic relationship with another adult.
- Understand that divorce will never lead to personal happiness.
- Move slowly in completing any legal separation papers.

D. Renewed Commitment

A renewed commitment after infidelity requires the recognition that true love is unconditional love; a love that puts the needs of the other before your own without condition. A vow renewal ceremony may be a way to express a renewed commitment between a husband and wife. If the choice is to be genuinely recommitted to the love confessed towards each other, there can be no condemnation. A renewed commitment takes discipline because we want to react out of our flesh. The intention of the spouse who has been hurt should never agree to a renewed commitment with the goal of subtly making the other spouse spend the rest of their life paying for the hurt they have caused. Genuine devotion to your spouse cannot be based on what satisfies you, but only strive to satisfy the interest of your spouse. We were born into sin and God offered His son as the Savior we needed for the forgiveness of our sins. We didn't have to do anything. There was no condition we had to meet. This is true love and it was a choice; therefore, love is a choice—not merely an emotion.

> *Love is patient, love is kind. It does not envy, it does not boast, it is not proud. 5It does not dishonor others, it is not self-seeking, it is not easily angered, it keeps no record of wrongs. 6Love does not delight in evil but rejoices with the truth. 7It always protects, always trusts, always hopes, always perseveres. 8Love never fails (1 Corinthians 13:4-8, NIV).*

Date_____

Dear God,

"But then one day I was brought into the sanctuaries

of God, and in the light of glory, my distorted

perspective vanished. Then I understood that the

destiny of the wicked was near!"

(Psalm 73:17 TPT).

_____

_____

_____

_____

_____

_____

_____

_____

_____

_____

_____

_____

_____

_____

_____

_____

I smile today because

V. Sexual Transparency

A. Choices

There hath no temptation taken you but such as is common to man: but God is faithful, who will not suffer you to be tempted above that ye are able; but will with the temptation also make a way to escape, that ye may be able to bear it (I Corinthians 10:13, KJV).

While it is important to understand that temptation is very real, it is just as important to understand that there is always a way out. This includes the hurt spouse who has made the choice to seek revenge sexually: having put themselves in a position of opportunity. This should never be the choice! Infidelity may not start off sexual and does not have to include sex to be considered as such. The potential for a strong emotional bond begins when a man and a woman share their hopes, dreams, plans, and even fears with each other rather than sharing them with their spouses. The element of secrecy added to the equation further enhances the bond as it satisfies a thrill created by the spirit of lust that "I am getting away with something." Adding sex to the equation takes the infidelity to a true place of danger; a place that can be very difficult to recover from as you try to move on sexually with your spouse.

The thoughts and visions of your spouse being intimate with someone else can feel like torture, further enhancing the fear to love freely. Although this may be a very scary place to be in and may take time to get through, as well as seeking professional/spiritual help, it is possible to achieve a renewed mind. Make the choice to ask God to give you the desire to be genuinely intimate with your spouse and their desire to be genuinely intimate with you. It is crucial not to just "go through the motions." Instead, share with your spouse the truth about the feelings you are experiencing. Genuinely make the choice to accept that the decisions your spouse made sexually don't have to haunt you from experiencing the intimacy God intended for a husband and wife. Choose to accept God's desire that *"marriage is honourable in all, and the bed undefiled: but whoremongers and adulterers God will judge"* *(Hebrews 13:4)*. Pray continually and be intentional about building and keeping a very healthy sexual relationship with your spouse from the very beginning of your marriage.

B. Effective Communication

Reviving your sexual relationship starts with openly communicating to your spouse what pleases you. Communicating openly about your sexual desires alleviates the burden of your spouse having to guess. This type of communication includes but not limited to, making requests, telling your spouse what feels pleasurable, and describing specific sexual desires (Subotnik, 2005). For example, sharing with your spouse that you just want to be held or that you like to be talked to a certain way while making love is essential to a fulfilling sexual relationship. Discovering these sexual likings of one another is key to accomplishing sexual compatibility—especially after infidelity. Openly communicating with your spouse is like a glimpse of the sun peeping through the rain clouds. Explore and have an adventurous sex life with your spouse. *"Be joyful in hope, patient in affliction, faithful in prayer" (Romans 12:12, NIV).*

Date_____

Dear God,

"When I saw all of this, what turmoil filled my heart,

piercing my opinions with your truth"

(Psalm 73:21 TPT).

_____

_____

_____

_____

_____

_____

_____

_____

_____

_____

_____

_____

_____

_____

_____

_____

I smile today because...

VI. Statistics

A. Divorce and Adultery

While adultery is no longer a deal breaker in many marriages, infidelity is one of the <u>top cited reasons</u> couples decide to get divorced.

- The experts at *Divorce Magazine* note that about 45-50 percent of married women and 50-60 percent of married men cheat on their spouses.

- According to the *American Psychological Association* (APA), infidelity in the United States accounted for 20-40 percent of divorces.

- The APA also cited that 42 percent of divorced individuals reported more than one affair.

- In a Gallup poll, researchers noted that more than half (sixty-two percent) of partners said they would leave their spouse and get a divorce if they found out their spouse was having an affair; thirty-one percent would stick it out and not divorce.

- However, in reality, *Divorce Magazine* notes that about 70 percent of couples actually stay together after an affair is discovered.

- Adultery is still one of the most cited reasons for divorce. According to a study published by the *National Institutes of Health*, one partner in 88 percent of couples studied cited infidelity as a major contributing factor. Interestingly, the vast majority of couples who divorced only had one partner share infidelity as a major issue.[11]

---

[11] Applebury, Gabrielle. "Rates of Divorce for Adultery and Infidelity." *LoveToKnow*, LoveToKnow Corp, https://divorce.lovetoknow.com/Rates_of_Divorce_for_Adultery_and_Infidelity.

B. Religion and Infidelity

Research examining the impact of religion on infidelity and divorce has illustrated that religiosity seems to increase the couple's happiness and therefore reduces the rate of divorce. They also found:

- Religion does not appear to have an effect on infidelity in couples who have been together for at least 12 years.

- Another study published in the *Journal of Divorce and Remarriage* indicated that for 21 percent of men, spirituality predicted their well-being after a divorce due to infidelity.

- A different study in the same journal noted that for 38 percent of women, spiritual well-being predicted divorce adjustment after spousal infidelity.[12]

---

[12] Applebury, Gabrielle. "Rates of Divorce for Adultery and Infidelity." *LoveToKnow,* LoveToKnow Corp,

https://divorce.lovetoknow.com/Rates_of_Divorce_for_Adultery_and _Infidelity.

VII. Interviews & Testimonies

A. Do You Think You Could Love Freely in Your Marriage After Being Hurt by Infidelity?

To my surprise, most of the testimonies shared had experienced infidelity in their marriage and were not able to trust again in that marriage, but with time, have been able to trust in marriages and relationships afterward. This was true of both men and women equally. One young lady shared how the infidelity in her marriage caused her to have low self-esteem. It took her a long time to learn to love herself. She allowed the infidelity to define her and felt she was not worthy of being loved because somehow it was "her fault." Today, she has a healthy marriage filled with fearless love for her husband because of her relationship with God. She has learned that God defines her, and she chooses to live by His standards.

B. How Has Infidelity Impacted Your Life Now?

The most memorable testimony given was of a story very similar to mine. The young lady shared that her youngest sister was the product of an affair her father had 12 years ago while married to her mother over 30 years. She recalled how her mother called her and her siblings to the family room where her father was wrapped around her mother's legs crying. She had never seen her father like that; he was their "superhero." He had gone through the deaths of his parents and she had never seen him so "completely broken." She stated her mother explained very calmly that their father was human and had made a mistake. However, they had a little sister who was not a mistake because she was "crafted by God." She was very adamant that she was a part of their family and if anyone ever treated her indifferently or with malice, she would "disown" them. She was also very adamant about not allowing other family members to treat her as an outsider and that she did not tolerate anyone who did. She describes her mother as a "warrior" and her parents are still going strong every day with God's help. This young lady's perspective on life is that giving up is too easy and allowing the "pain and transgressions against you be an excuse." With constant work and a decision to keep fighting, she has witnessed genuine repentance and genuine forgiveness.

Date_____

Thank you, Father God,

"I will give you a new heart and put a new spirit in

you; I will remove from you your heart of stone and

give you a heart of flesh"

(Ezekiel 36:26 NIV).

_____

_____

_____

_____

_____

_____

_____

_____

_____

_____

_____

_____

_____

_____

_____

_____

_____

I smile today because...

VIII. Setting Boundaries

A. Should You Set Boundaries with Your Spouse?

[13]"A healthy, thriving marriage is like a grapevine or a garden: to a certain extent, it needs to be walled in and protected from outside influences that might pose a threat to its continued growth and fruitfulness." Marriage can come under attack in various ways. The relationship loses its strength and in a matter of time, it deteriorates. Husbands and wives become confused and there is an emotional disconnect. This is the perfect scene for couples to seek for connection outside of their marriage. The chance is greatly reduced when care is invested into setting boundaries in your marriage. For example,

---

[13] www.focusonthefamily.com

having opposite-sex friends may not be wise despite how long-term of a friendship it may be. If your spouse is not accepting of the friendship, this supersedes the friendship, and you are obligated to respect how your spouse feels. The goal is to not just have a marriage that lasts, but one that flourishes.

B. Addressing the Fear

"Watch and pray so that you will not fall into temptation. The spirit is willing, but the flesh is weak" (Matthew 26:41). "I'm so afraid of being hurt again. I'm so afraid of my family never being the same." Had we failed our children? Part of me wanted to let my guard down, but I just couldn't. I wanted to genuinely smile without feeling as though "if I smile too much, he might think I forgot what he did." I wanted our bed to be completely undefiled, but would it be enjoyable enough for him? But I had forgiven,

right!? I said I did. There were days I felt I did, but truthfully, I was so afraid to just let myself love my husband the way I really wanted to because I did not fully trust him. I knew he loved me. God showed me his sorrow was genuine, but I could not bring myself to fully trust him. Was he really going to the store? Did he call or text her when he went? If I have forgiven and say I trusted him, this means I shouldn't check his phone, right? But what about those "boundaries" that I can set because they are just as important after infidelity? How will I really know if I don't check?

These are the types of conversations I had with myself before I decided (with the help of the Holy Spirit) that I would look to God for the trust and not my husband. It was very clear to the both of us that God had restored our marriage to its rightful place.

Therefore, trusting God did not mean I had to turn a blind eye or accept any type of disrespect; it simply meant to me that I had to believe that trusting my husband would be found in having complete faith in the One who created him. This was my turning point of overcoming the fear to love freely.

C. Expectancy

"Do I want my marriage to survive?" There are times we must face things head-on for what they are and allow the answer to the question propel us to the next step. This may be the only way you will truly decide how to proceed. This question must be asked and answered by the spouse who has been hurt as well as the unfaithful spouse. The answer should be answered honestly and shared with one another. More than likely, the spouse who has been hurt is looking for signs of survival rather than just words. However, it is equally important to accept the fact that if the unfaithful spouse desires survival also, they are looking for signs as well. As difficult as it may be, the hurt spouse should be considerate of the shattered feeling their spouse may be experiencing. It is beneficial that your spouse has an expectancy of themselves to work diligently toward a surviving and thriving marriage.

Your marriage will survive infidelity if:

- You are working on rebuilding trust.
- Your spouse is committed to rebuilding trust.
- You can stomach uncomfortable conversations.
- You can talk openly about the affair.
- You are confident in and out of the bed.
- You and your spouse know how to talk about regret.

- You never use the term "Get over it."

- You are comfortable expressing anger and sorrow.

- You and your spouse are invested in activities together.

- You are open to counseling.

- You are up to evaluating your relationship before and after the affair.

- You are willing to give up passwords to phones and other electronics.

- You're not interested in playing the "blame game."

- You are empathetic.

- You know when to stop asking questions.[14]

---

[14] "15 Signs Your Marriage Will Survive Infidelity." Romper, https://www.romper.com/p/15-signs-your-marriage-will-survive-infidelity-14375/amp.

Date_____

Dear God,

"Yet, in spite of all this, you comfort me by your

counsel; you draw me closer to you. You lead me

with your secret wisdom. And following you brings

me into your brightness and glory"

(Psalm 73:23-24 TPT)!

_____

_____

_____

_____

_____

_____

_____

_____

_____

_____

_____

_____

_____

_____

_____

_____

_____

I smile today because...

IX. Conclusion

A New Beginnings

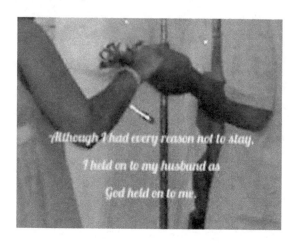

"Now the Lord is the Spirit, and where the Spirit of

the Lord is, there is freedom"

(2 Corinthians 3:17 NIV).

I overcame the fear to love my husband freely

because Jesus would not let me go! I cried out to God

to take the pain away, only to conclude that His grace

is sufficient. Today, we not only understand the value

of our [15]roles as husband and wife, but we are intentional about respecting them. We are honored to be of the same flesh and are very grateful God has ordained it as such. I literally felt my husband's brokenness and soon realized that he needed me to get through his pain as I depended on God to get us through. This journey has not been easy, but with God, all things are truly possible. Following the Holy Spirit will lead you to freedom. He fights for us all!

Our love story...

"Place me like a seal over your heart, like a seal on your arm; for love is as strong as death, its jealousy unyielding as the grave. It burns like blazing fire, like a mighty flame. Many waters cannot quench love;

---

[15] 1 Corinthians 11:3, Ephesians 5:22-24; 5:25-26;28-29, 33

rivers cannot sweep it away. If one were to give all the wealth of one's house for love, it would be utterly scorned" (Song of Songs 8:6-7 NIV).

Date_____

Dear God,

"Lord, so many times I fail; I fall into disgrace.

But when I trust in you, I have a strong and glorious

presence protecting and anointing me.

Forever you're all I need"

(Psalm 73:26 TPT)!

_____

_____

_____

_____

_____

_____

_____

_____

_____

_____

_____

_____

_____

_____

_____

_____

_____

I smile today because...

Bibliography

Applebury, G. (n.d.). *Rates of Divorce for Adultery and Infidelity*. Retrieved from Love to Know. https://divorce.lovetoknow.com/Rates_of_Divorce_for_Adultery_and_Infidelity.

Beall, C. (2011). *Healing Your Marriage When Trust is Broken*. Harvest House Publisher.

Beall, C. (2016). *Rebuilding a Marriage Better Than New*. Harvest House Publisher.

Chapman, G. (2018). *Loving Your Spouse When You Feel Like Walking Away*. Moody Publishers.

Bevere, J. (1994). *The Bait of Satan*. Charisma House.

Desai, Amy. "How Could Divorce Affect My Kids?" *Focus On the Family*, 1 January 2007. https://www.focusonthefamily.com/marriage/divorce-and-infidelity/should-i-get-a-divorce/how-could-divorce-affect-my-kids.

Donato, D. (2016, July 2016). *15 Signs Your Marriage Will Survive Infidelity*. Retrieved from Romper.com: https://www.romper.com/p/15-signs-your-marriage-will-survive-infideli ty-14375/amp

MacArthur, J. (2008). *The Truth War: Fighting for certainty in an Age of Deception*. Thomas Nelson.

Millard, A. F. (2013). *The Hurt and the Healer*. Grand Rapids: Baxter Publishing Group.

Rosenberg, G. a. (2002). *Healing the Hurt in Your Marriage.* Tyndale House Publishers, Inc.

Subotnik, Rona B.. *Surviving Infidelity: Making Decisions, Recovering from the Pain* (Kindle Location 1813). Adams Media. Kindle Edition.